EDNA ST. VINCENT MILLAY'S
POEMS

SELECTED FOR YOUNG PEOPLE

EDNA ST. VINCENT MILLAY'S

POEMS

SELECTED FOR YOUNG PEOPLE

Woodcuts by Ronald Keller

Harper & Row, Publishers

Edna St. Vincent Millay's Poems Selected for Young People
Text copyright, 1917, 1921, 1922, 1923, 1929, 1949, 1950, 1951,
by Edna St. Vincent Millay. Copyright, 1951, by Norma Millay Ellis.
Illustrations copyright © 1979 by Ronald Keller.
New edition

Library of Congress Cataloging in Publication Data
Millay, Edna St. Vincent, 1892–1950.
    Edna St. Vincent Millay's poems selected for
young people.

    SUMMARY: A selection of poems by Edna St.
Vincent Millay especially chosen for young people.
    [1. American poetry]   I. Keller, Ronald.
II. Title.   III. Title: Poems selected for young
people.
PS3525.I495P65 1979   811'.5'2   77–25671
ISBN 0-06-024218-3
ISBN 0-06-024219-1 lib. bdg.

CONTENTS

PART THREE

PART FOUR

PART FIVE

PART SIX

Sonnets

PART ONE

From a Very Little Sphinx

I

Come along in then, little girl!
Or else stay out!
But in the open door she stands,
And bites her lip and twists her hands,
And stares upon me, trouble-eyed:
"Mother," she says, "I can't decide!
I can't decide!"

II

Oh, burdock, and you other dock,
That have ground coffee for your seeds,
And lovely long thin daisies, dear—
She said that you are weeds!
She said, "Oh, what a fine bouquet!"
But afterwards I heard her say,
"She's always dragging in those weeds."

III

Everybody but just me
Despises burdocks. Mother, she
Despises 'em the most because
They stick so to my socks and drawers.
But father, when he sits on some,
Can't speak a decent word for 'em.

IV

I know a hundred ways to die.
I've often thought I'd try one:
Lie down beneath a motor truck
Some day when standing by one.

Or throw myself from off a bridge—
Except such things must be
So hard upon the scavengers
And men that clean the sea.

I know some poison I could drink.
I've often thought I'd taste it.
But mother bought it for the sink,
And drinking it would waste it.

V

Look, Edwin! Do you see that boy
Talking to the other boy?
No, over there by those two men—
Wait, don't look now—now look again.
No, not the one in navy-blue;
That's the one he's talking to.
Sure you see him? Stripèd pants?
Well, *he was born in Paris, France.*

VI

All the grown-up people say,
"What, those ugly thistles?
Mustn't touch them! Keep away!
Prickly! Full of bristles!"

Yet they never make me bleed
Half so much as roses!
Must be purple is a weed,
And pink and white is posies.

VII

Wonder where this horseshoe went.
Up and down, up and down,
Up and past the monument,
Maybe into town.

Wait a minute.   "Horseshoe,
How far have you been?"
Says it's been to Salem
And halfway to Lynn.

Wonder who was in the team.
Wonder what they saw.
Wonder if they passed a bridge—
Bridge with a draw.

Says it went from one bridge
Straight upon another.
Says it took a little girl
Driving with her mother.

Afternoon on a Hill

I will be the gladdest thing
    Under the sun!
I will touch a hundred flowers
    And not pick one.

I will look at cliffs and clouds
    With quiet eyes,
Watch the wind bow down the grass,
    And the grass rise.

And when lights begin to show
    Up from the town,
I will mark which must be mine,
    And then start down!

City Trees

The trees along this city street,
   Save for the traffic and the trains,
Would make a sound as thin and sweet
   As trees in country lanes.

And people standing in their shade
   Out of a shower, undoubtedly
Would hear such music as is made
   Upon a country tree.

Oh, little leaves that are so dumb
   Against the shrieking city air,
I watch you when the wind has come,—
   I know what sound is there.

The Blue-Flag in the Bog

God had called us, and we came;
   Our loved Earth to ashes left;
Heaven was a neighbor's house,
   Open flung to us, bereft.

Gay the lights of Heaven showed,
   And 'twas God who walked ahead;
Yet I wept along the road,
   Wanting my own house instead.

Wept unseen, unheeded cried,
   "All you things my eyes have kissed,
Fare you well! We meet no more,
   Lovely, lovely tattered mist!

Weary wings that rise and fall
   All day long above the fire!"—
Red with heat was every wall,
   Rough with heat was every wire—

"Fare you well, you little winds
   That the flying embers chase!
Fare you well, you shuddering day,
   With your hands before your face!

And, ah, blackened by strange blight,
   Or to a false sun unfurled,
Now forevermore goodbye,
   All the gardens in the world!

On the windless hills of Heaven,
   That I have no wish to see,
White, eternal lilies stand,
   By a lake of ebony.

But the Earth forevermore
   Is a place where nothing grows,—
Dawn will come, and no bud break;
   Evening, and no blossom close.

Spring will come, and wander slow
   Over an indifferent land,
Stand beside an empty creek,
   Hold a dead seed in her hand."

God had called us, and we came,
   But the blessed road I trod
Was a bitter road to me,
   And at heart I questioned God.

"Though in Heaven," I said, "be all
   That the heart would most desire,
Held Earth naught save souls of sinners
   Worth the saving from a fire?

Withered grass,—the wasted growing!
   Aimless ache of laden boughs!"
Little things God had forgotten
   Called me, from my burning house.

"Though in Heaven," I said, "be all
   That the eye could ask to see,
All the things I ever knew
   Are this blaze in back of me.

"Though in Heaven," I said, "be all
    That the ear could think to lack,
All the things I ever knew
    Are this roaring at my back."

It was God who walked ahead,
    Like a shepherd to the fold;
In his footsteps fared the weak,
    And the weary and the old,

Glad enough of gladness over,
    Ready for the peace to be,—
But a thing God had forgotten
    Was the growing bones of me.

And I drew a bit apart,
    And I lagged a bit behind,
And I thought on Peace Eternal,
    Lest He look into my mind:

And I gazed up on the sky,
    And I thought of Heavenly Rest,—
And I slipped away like water
    Through the fingers of the blest!

All their eyes were fixed on Glory.
    Not a glance brushed over me;
"Alleluia!   Alleluia!"
    Up the road,—and I was free.

And my heart rose like a freshet,
    And it swept me on before,
Giddy as a whirling stick,
    Till I felt the earth once more.

All the Earth was charred and black,
   Fire had swept from pole to pole;
And the bottom of the sea
   Was as brittle as a bowl;

And the timbered mountain-top
   Was as naked as a skull,—
Nothing left, nothing left,
   Of the Earth so beautiful!

"Earth," I said, "how can I leave you?"
   "You are all I have," I said;
"What is left to take my mind up,
   Living always, and you dead?"

"Speak!" I said. "Oh, tell me something!
   Make a sign that I can see!
For a keepsake! To keep always!
   Quick!—before God misses me!"

And I listened for a voice;—
   But my heart was all I heard;
Not a screech-owl, not a loon,
   Not a tree-toad said a word.

And I waited for a sign;—
   Coals and cinders, nothing more;
And a little cloud of smoke
   Floating on a valley floor.

And I peered into the smoke
   Till it rotted, like a fog:—
There, encompassed round by fire,
   Stood a blue-flag in a bog!

Little flames came wading out,
    Straining, straining towards its stem,
But it was so blue and tall
    That it scorned to think of them!

Red and thirsty were their tongues,
    As the tongues of wolves must be,
But it was so blue and tall—
    Oh, I laughed, I cried, to see!

All my heart became a tear,
　All my soul became a tower,
Never loved I anything
　As I loved that tall blue flower!

It was all the little boats
　That had ever sailed the sea,
It was all the little books
　That had gone to school with me;

On its roots like iron claws
  Rearing up so blue and tall,—
It was all the gallant Earth
  With its back against a wall!

In a breath, ere I had breathed—
  Oh, I laughed, I cried, to see!—
I was kneeling at its side,
  And it leaned its head on me!

Crumbling stones and sliding sand
  Is the road to Heaven now;
Icy at my straining knees
  Drags the awful under-tow;

Soon but stepping-stones of dust
  Will the road to Heaven be,—
Father, Son and Holy Ghost,
  Reach a hand and rescue me!

"There—there, my blue-flag flower;
  Hush—hush—go to sleep;
That is only God you hear,
  Counting up His folded sheep!

Lullabye—lullabye—
  That is only God that calls,
Missing me, seeking me,
  Ere the road to nothing falls!

He will set His mighty feet
    Firmly on the sliding sand;
Like a little frightened bird
    I will creep into His hand;

I will tell Him all my grief,
    I will tell Him all my sin;
He will give me half His robe
    For a cloak to wrap you in.

Lullabye—lullabye—"
    Rocks the burnt-out planet free!
Father, Son and Holy Ghost,
    Reach a hand and rescue me!

Ah, the voice of love at last!
    Lo, at last the face of light!
And the whole of His white robe
    For a cloak against the night!

And upon my heart asleep
    All the things I ever knew!—
"Holds Heaven not some cranny, Lord,
    For a flower so tall and blue?"

All's well and all's well!
    Gay the lights of Heaven show!
In some moist and Heavenly place
    We will set it out to grow.

Journey

Ah, could I lay me down in this long grass
And close my eyes, and let the quiet wind
Blow over me,—I am so tired, so tired
Of passing pleasant places!   All my life,
Following Care along the dusty road,
Have I looked back at loveliness and sighed;
Yet at my hand an unrelenting hand
Tugged ever, and I passed.   All my life long
Over my shoulder have I looked at peace;
And now I fain would lie in this long grass
And close my eyes.
                        Yet onward!
                                    Cat-birds call
Through the long afternoon, and creeks at dusk
Are guttural.   Whip-poor-wills wake and cry,
Drawing the twilight close about their throats.
Only my heart makes answer.   Eager vines
Go up the rocks and wait; flushed apple-trees
Pause in their dance and break the ring for me;
Dim, shady wood-roads, redolent of fern
And bayberry, that through sweet bevies thread
Of round-faced roses, pink and petulant,
Look back and beckon ere they disappear.
Only my heart, only my heart responds.
Yet, ah, my path is sweet on either side
All through the dragging day,—sharp underfoot,
And hot, and like dead mist the dry dust hangs—
But far, oh, far as passionate eye can reach,

And long, ah, long as rapturous eye can cling,
The world is mine: blue hill, still silver lake,
Broad field, bright flower, and the long white road
A gateless garden, and an open path:
My feet to follow, and my heart to hold.

Eel-Grass

No matter what I say,
　All that I really love
Is the rain that flattens on the bay,
　And the eel-grass in the cove;
The jingle-shells that lie and bleach
　At the tide-line, and the trace
Of higher tides along the beach:
　Nothing in this place.

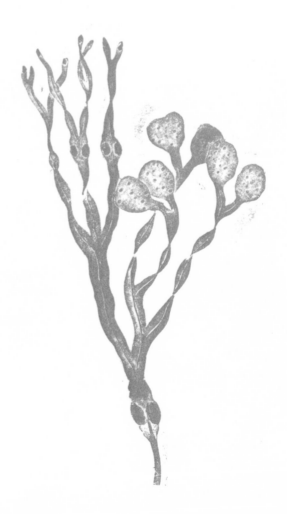

God's World

O world, I cannot hold thee close enough!
   Thy winds, thy wide grey skies!
   Thy mists, that roll and rise!
Thy woods, this autumn day, that ache and sag
And all but cry with colour! That gaunt crag
To crush! To lift the lean of that black bluff!
World, World, I cannot get thee close enough!

Long have I known a glory in it all,
     But never knew I this;
     Here such a passion is
As stretcheth me apart,—Lord, I do fear
Thou'st made the world too beautiful this year;
My soul is all but out of me,—let fall
No burning leaf; prithee, let no bird call.

Pastoral

If it were only still!—
With far away the shrill
Crying of a cock;
Or the shaken bell
From a cow's throat
Moving through the bushes;
Or the soft shock
Of wizened apples falling
From an old tree
In a forgotten orchard
Upon the hilly rock!

Oh, grey hill,
Where the grazing herd
Licks the purple blossom,
Crops the spiky weed!
Oh, stony pasture,
Where the tall mullein
Stands up so sturdy
On its little seed!

Assault

I

I had forgotten how the frogs must sound
After a year of silence, else I think
I should not so have ventured forth alone
At dusk upon this unfrequented road.

II

I am waylaid by Beauty.   Who will walk
Between me and the crying of the frogs?
Oh, savage Beauty, suffer me to pass,
That am a timid woman, on her way
From one house to another!

Low-Tide

These wet rocks where the tide has been,
  Barnacled white and weeded brown
And slimed beneath to a beautiful green,
  These wet rocks where the tide went down
Will show again when the tide is high,
  Faint and perilous, far from shore,
No place to dream, but a place to die,—
  The bottom of the sea once more.
There was a child that wandered through
  A giant's empty house all day,—
House full of wonderful things and new,
  But no fit place for a child to play.

Song of a Second April

April this year, not otherwise
  Than April of a year ago,
Is full of whispers, full of sighs,
  Of dazzling mud and dingy snow;
  Hepaticas that pleased you so
Are here again, and butterflies.

There rings a hammering all day,
  And shingles lie about the doors;
In orchards near and far away
  The grey wood-pecker taps and bores;
  And men are merry at their chores,
And children earnest at their play.

The larger streams run still and deep,
  Noisy and swift the small brooks run
Among the mullein stalks the sheep
  Go up the hillside in the sun,
  Pensively,—only you are gone,
You that alone I cared to keep.

10⁸

Inland

People that build their houses inland,
   People that buy a plot of ground
Shaped like a house, and build a house there,
   Far from the sea-board, far from the sound

Of water sucking the hollow ledges,
   Tons of water striking the shore,—
What do they long for, as I long for
   One salt smell of the sea once more?

People the waves have not awakened,
   Spanking the boats at the harbour's head,
What do they long for, as I long for,—
   Starting up in my inland bed,

Beating the narrow walls, and finding
   Neither a window nor a door,
Screaming to God for death by drowning,—
   One salt taste of the sea once more?

144

Doubt No More That Oberon

Doubt no more that Oberon—
Never doubt that Pan
Lived, and played a reed, and ran
After nymphs in a dark forest,
In the merry, credulous days,—
Lived, and led a fairy band
Over the indulgent land!
Ah, for in this dourest, sorest
Age man's eye has looked upon,
Death to fauns and death to fays,
Still the dog-wood dares to raise—
Healthy tree, with trunk and root—
Ivory bowls that bear no fruit,
And the starlings and the jays—
Birds that cannot even sing—
Dare to come again in spring!

Exiled

Searching my heart for its true sorrow,
  This is the thing I find to be:
That I am weary of words and people
  Sick of the city, wanting the sea;

Wanting the sticky, salty sweetness
  Of the strong wind and shattered spray;
Wanting the loud sound and the soft sound
  Of the big surf that breaks all day.

Always before about my dooryard,
  Marking the reach of the winter sea,
Rooted in sand and dragging drift-wood,
  Straggled the purple wild sweet-pea; ·

Always I climbed the wave at morning,
  Shook the sand from my shoes at night,
That now am caught beneath great buildings,
  Stricken with noise, confused with light.

If I could hear the green piles groaning
    Under the windy wooden piers,
See once again the bobbing barrels,
    And the black sticks that fence the weirs.

If I could see the weedy mussels
    Crusting the wrecked and rotting hulls,
Hear once again the hungry crying
    Overhead, of the wheeling gulls,

Feel once again the shanty straining
    Under the turning of the tide,
Fear once again the rising freshet,
    Dread the bell in the fog outside,—

I should be happy,—that was happy
    All day long on the coast of Maine!
I have a need to hold and handle
    Shells and anchors and ships again!

I should be happy, that am happy
    Never at all since I came here.
I am too long away from water.
    I have a need of water near.

Alms

My heart is what it was before,
  A house where people come and go;
But it is winter with your love,
  The sashes are beset with snow.

I light the lamp and lay the cloth,
  I blow the coals to blaze again;
But it is winter with your love,
  The frost is thick upon the pane.

I know a winter when it comes:
  The leaves are listless on the boughs;
I watched your love a little while,
  And brought my plants into the house.

I water them and turn them south,
  I snap the dead brown from the stem;
But it is winter with your love,—
  I only tend and water them.

There was a time I stood and watched
  The small, ill-natured sparrows' fray;
I loved the beggar that I fed,
  I cared for what he had to say,

I stood and watched him out of sight;
  Today I reach around the door
And set a bowl upon the step;
  My heart is what it was before,

But it is winter with your love;
   I scatter crumbs upon the sill,
And close the window,—and the birds
   May take or leave them, as they will.

Autumn Chant

Now the autumn shudders
  In the rose's root.
Far and wide the ladders
  Lean among the fruit.

Now the autumn clambers
  Up the trellised frame,
And the rose remembers
  The dust from which it came.

Brighter than the blossom
  On the rose's bough
Sits the wizened orange,
  Bitter berry now;

Beauty never slumbers;
  All is in her name;
But the rose remembers
  The dust from which it came.

Nuit Blanche

I am a shepherd of those sheep
   That climb a wall by night,
One after one, until I sleep,
   Or the black pane goes white
Because of which I cannot see
   A flock upon a hill,
But doubts come tittering up to me
   That should by day be still.
And childish griefs I have outgrown
   Into my eyes are thrust,
Till my dull tears go dropping down
   Like lead into the dust.

The Wood Road

If I were to walk this way
  Hand in hand with Grief,
I should mark that maple-spray
  Coming into leaf.
I should note how the old burrs
  Rot upon the ground.
Yes, though Grief should know me hers
  While the world goes round,
It could not in truth be said
  This was lost on me:
A rock-maple showing red,
  Burrs beneath a tree.

The Spring and the Fall

In the spring of the year, in the spring of the year
I walked the road beside my dear.
The trees were black where the bark was wet.
I see them yet, in the spring of the year.
He broke me a bough of the blossoming peach
That was out of the way and hard to reach.

In the fall of the year, in the fall of the year,
I walked the road beside my dear.
The rooks went up with a raucous trill.
I hear them still, in the fall of the year.
He laughed at all I dared to praise,
And broke my heart, in little ways.

Year be springing or year be falling,
The bark will drip and the birds be calling.
There's much that's fine to see and hear
In the spring of a year, in the fall of a year.
'Tis not love's going hurts my days,
But that it went in little ways.

PART TWO

First Fig

My candle burns at both ends;
  It will not last the night;
But ah, my foes, and oh, my friends—
  It gives a lovely light!

Second Fig

Safe upon the solid rock the ugly houses stand:
Come and see my shining palace built upon the sand!

To the Not Impossible Him

How shall I know, unless I go
  To Cairo and Cathay,
Whether or not this blessed spot
  Is blest in every way?

Now it may be, the flower for me
  Is this beneath my nose;
How shall I tell, unless I smell
  The Carthaginian rose?

The fabric of my faithful love
  No power shall dim or ravel
Whilst I stay here,—but oh, my dear,
  If I should ever travel!

Recuerdo

We were very tired, we were very merry—
We had gone back and forth all night on the ferry.
It was bare and bright, and smelled like a stable—
But we looked into a fire, we leaned across a table,
We lay on the hill-top underneath the moon;
And the whistles kept blowing, and the dawn came soon.

We were very tired, we were very merry—
We had gone back and forth all night on the ferry;
And you ate an apple, and I ate a pear,
From a dozen of each we had bought somewhere;
And the sky went wan, and the wind came cold,
And the sun rose dripping, a bucketful of gold.

We were very tired, we were very merry—
We had gone back and forth all night on the ferry.
We hailed, "Good morrow, mother!" to a shawl-covered
        head,
And bought a morning paper, which neither of us read;
And she wept, "God bless you!" for the apples and the
        pears,
And we gave her all our money but our subway fares.

The Unexplorer

There was a road ran past our house
Too lovely to explore.
I asked my mother once—she said
That if you followed where it led
It brought you to the milk-man's door.
(That's why I have not traveled more.)

Grown-Up

Was it for this I uttered prayers,
And sobbed and cursed and kicked the stairs,
That now, domestic as a plate,
I should retire at half-past eight?

Daphne

Why do you follow me?—
Any moment I can be
Nothing but a laurel-tree.

Any moment of the chase
I can leave you in my place
A pink bough for your embrace.

Yet if over hill and hollow
Still it is your will to follow,
I am off;—to heel, Apollo!

The Philosopher

And what are you that, missing you,
   I should be kept awake
As many nights as there are days
   With weeping for your sake?

And what are you that, missing you,
   As many days as crawl
I should be listening to the wind
   And looking at the wall?

I know a man that's a braver man
   And twenty men as kind,
And what are you, that you should be
   The one man in my mind?

Yet women's ways are witless ways,
   As any sage will tell,—
And what am I, that I should love
   So wisely and so well?

Travel

The railroad track is miles away,
  And the day is loud with voices speaking,
Yet there isn't a train goes by all day
  But I hear its whistle shrieking.

All night there isn't a train goes by,
  Though the night is still for sleep and dreaming,
But I see its cinders red on the sky,
  And hear its engine steaming.

My heart is warm with the friends I make,
  And better friends I'll not be knowing,
Yet there isn't a train I wouldn't take,
  No matter where it's going.

Rosemary

For the sake of some things
  That be now no more
I will strew rushes
  On my chamber-floor,
I will plant bergamot
  At my kitchen-door.

For the sake of dim things
  That were once so plain
I will set a barrel
  Out to catch the rain,
I will hang an iron pot
  On an iron crane.

Many things be dead and gone
  That were brave and gay;
For the sake of these things
  I will learn to say,
"An it please you, gentle sirs,"
  "Alack!" and "Well-a-day!"

Ebb

I know what my heart is like
Since your love died:
It is like a hollow ledge
Holding a little pool
  Left there by the tide,
  A little tepid pool,
Drying inward from the edge.

The Little Hill

Oh, here the air is sweet and still,
  And soft's the grass to lie on;
And far away's the little hill
  They took for Christ to die on.

And there's a hill across the brook,
  And down the brook's another;
But, oh, the little hill they took,—
  I think I am its mother!

The moon that saw Gethsemane,
  I watch it rise and set;
It has so many things to see,
  They help it to forget.

But little hills that sit at home
  So many hundred years,
Remember Greece, remember Rome,
  Remember Mary's tears.

And far away in Palestine,
  Sadder than any other,
Grieves still the hill that I call mine,—
  I think I am its mother!

160

Wild Swans

I looked in my heart while the wild swans went over.
And what did I see I had not seen before?
Only a question less or a question more;
Nothing to match the flight of wild birds flying.
Tiresome heart, forever living and dying,
House without air, I leave you and lock your door
Wild swans, come over the town, come over
The town again, trailing your legs and crying!

Sorrow

Sorrow like a ceaseless rain
Beats upon my heart.
People twist and scream in pain,—
Dawn will find them still again;
This has neither wax nor wane,
  Neither stop nor start.

People dress and go to town;
  I sit in my chair.
All my thoughts are slow and brown:
Standing up or sitting down
Little matters, or what gown
  Or what shoes I wear.

Elaine

Oh, come again to Astolat!
I will not ask you to be kind.
And you may go when you will go,
And I will stay behind.

I will not say how dear you are,
Or ask you if you hold me dear,
Or trouble you with things for you
The way I did last year.

So still the orchard, Lancelot,
So very still the lake shall be,
You could not guess—though you should guess—
What is become of me.

So wide shall be the garden-walk,
The garden-seat so very wide,
You needs must think—if you should think—
The lily maid had died.

Save that, a little way away,
I'd watch you for a little while,
To see you speak, the way you speak,
And smile—if you should smile.

Souvenir

Just a rainy day or two
In a windy tower,
That was all I had of you—
Saving half an hour

Marred by greeting passing groups
In a cinder walk,
Near some naked blackberry hoops
Dim with purple chalk.

I remember three or four
Things you said in spite,
And an ugly coat you wore,
Plaided black and white.

Just a rainy day or two
And a bitter word.
Why do I remember you
As a singing bird?

Scrub

If I grow bitterly,
Like a gnarled and stunted tree,
Bearing harshly of my youth
Puckered fruit that sears the mouth;
If I make of my drawn boughs
An inhospitable house,
Out of which I never pry
Towards the water and the sky,
Under which I stand and hide
And hear the day go by outside;
It is that a wind too strong
Bent my back when I was young,
It is that I fear the rain
Lest it blister me again.

Departure

It's little I care what path I take,
And where it leads it's little I care;
But out of this house, lest my heart break,
I must go, and off somewhere.

It's little I know what's in my heart,
What's in my mind it's little I know,
But there's that in me must up and start,
And it's little I care where my feet go.

I wish I could walk for a day and a night,
And find me at dawn in a desolate place
With never the rut of a road in sight,
Nor the roof of a house, nor the eyes of a face.

I wish I could walk till my blood should spout
And drop me, never to stir again,
On a shore that is wide, for the tide is out,
And the weedy rocks are bare to the rain.

But dump or dock, where the path I take
Brings up, it's little enough I care;
And it's little I'd mind the fuss they'll make,
Huddled dead in a ditch somewhere.

"Is something the matter, dear," she said,
"That you sit at your work so silently?"
"No, mother, no, 'twas a knot in my thread:
There goes the kettle, I'll make the tea."

The Curse

Oh, lay my ashes on the wind
That blows across the sea.
And I shall meet a fisherman
Out of Capri,

And he will say, seeing me,
"What a strange thing!
Like a fish's scale or a
Butterfly's wing."

Oh, lay my ashes on the wind
That blows away the fog.
And I shall meet a farmer boy
Leaping through the bog,

And he will say, seeing me,
"What a strange thing!
Like a peat-ash or a
Butterfly's wing."

And I shall blow to your house
And, sucked against the pane,
See you take your sewing up
And lay it down again.

And you will say, seeing me,
"What a strange thing!
Like a plum petal or a
Butterfly's wing."

And none at all will know me
That knew me well before
But I will settle at the root
That climbs about your door,

And fishermen and farmers
May see me and forget,
But I'll be a bitter berry
In your brewing yet.

The Little Ghost

I knew her for a little ghost
   That in my garden walked;
The wall is high—higher than most—
   And the green gate was locked.

And yet I did not think of that
   Till after she was gone—
I knew her by the broad white hat,
   All ruffled, she had on.

By the dear ruffles round her feet,
   By her small hands that hung
In their lace mitts, austere and sweet,
   Her gown's white folds among.

I watched to see if she would stay,
   What she would do—and oh!
She looked as if she liked the way
   I let my garden grow!

She bent above my favourite mint
   With conscious garden grace,
She smiled and smiled—there was no hint
   Of sadness in her face.

She held her gown on either side
   To let her slippers show,
And up the walk she went with pride,
   The way great ladies go.

And where the walk is built in new
  And is of ivy bare
She paused—then opened and passed through
  A gate that once was there.

PART THREE

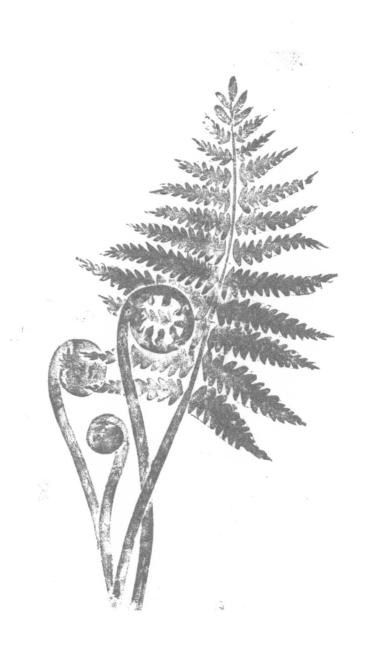

Renascence

All I could see from where I stood
Was three long mountains and a wood;
I turned and looked another way,
And saw three islands in a bay.
So with my eyes I traced the line
Of the horizon, thin and fine,
Straight around till I was come
Back to where I'd started from;
And all I saw from where I stood
Was three long mountains and a wood.
Over these things I could not see:
These were the things that bounded me;
And I could touch them with my hand,
Almost, I thought, from where I stand.
And all at once things seemed so small
My breath came short, and scarce at all.
But, sure, the sky is big, I said;
Miles and miles above my head;
So here upon my back I'll lie
And look my fill into the sky.
And so I looked, and, after all,
The sky was not so very tall.
The sky, I said, must somewhere stop,
And—sure enough!—I see the top!
The sky, I thought, is not so grand;
I 'most could touch it with my hand!
And reaching up my hand to try,
I screamed to feel it touch the sky.
I screamed, and—lo!—Infinity
Came down and settled over me;

Forced back my scream into my chest,
Bent back my arm upon my breast,
And, pressing of the Undefined
The definition on my mind,
Held up before my eyes a glass
Through which my shrinking sight did pass
Until it seemed I must behold
Immensity made manifold;
Whispered to me a word whose sound
Deafened the air for worlds around,
And brought unmuffled to my ears
The gossiping of friendly spheres,
The creaking of the tented sky,
The ticking of Eternity.

I saw and heard and knew at last
The How and Why of all things, past,
And present, and forevermore.
The Universe, cleft to the core,
Lay open to my probing sense
That, sick'ning, I would fain pluck thence
But could not,—nay!   But needs must suck
At the great wound, and could not pluck
My lips away till I had drawn
All venom out.—Ah, fearful pawn!
For my omniscience paid I toll
In infinite remorse of soul.
All sin was of my sinning, all
Atoning mine, and mine the gall
Of all regret.   Mine was the weight
Of every brooded wrong, the hate
That stood behind each envious thrust,
Mine every greed, mine every lust.
And all the while for every grief,
Each suffering, I craved relief
With individual desire,—
Craved all in vain!   And felt fierce fire
About a thousand people crawl;
Perished with each,—then mourned for all!
A man was starving in Capri;
He moved his eyes and looked at me;
I felt his gaze, I heard his moan,
And knew his hunger as my own.
I saw at sea a great fog bank
Between two ships that struck and sank;
A thousand screams the heavens smote;
And every scream tore through my throat.

No hurt I did not feel, no death
That was not mine; mine each last breath
That, crying, met an answering cry
From the compassion that was I.
All suffering mine, and mine its rod;
Mine, pity like the pity of God.
Ah, awful weight!   Infinity
Pressed down upon the finite Me!
My anguished spirit, like a bird,
Beating against my lips I heard;
Yet lay the weight so close about
There was no room for it without.
And so beneath the weight lay I
And suffered death, but could not die.

Long had I lain thus, craving death,
When quietly the earth beneath
Gave way, and inch by inch, so great
At last had grown the crushing weight,
Into the earth I sank till I
Full six feet under ground did lie,
And sank no more,—there is no weight
Can follow here, however great.
From off my breast I felt it roll,
And as it went my tortured soul
Burst forth and fled in such a gust
That all about me swirled the dust.

Deep in the earth I rested now;
Cool is its hand upon the brow
And soft its breast beneath the head
Of one who is so gladly dead.

And all at once, and over all
The pitying rain began to fall;
I lay and heard each pattering hoof
Upon my lowly, thatchèd roof,
And seemed to love the sound far more
Than ever I had done before.
For rain it hath a friendly sound
To one who's six feet under ground;
And scarce the friendly voice or face:
A grave is such a quiet place.

The rain, I said, is kind to come
And speak to me in my new home.
I would I were alive again
To kiss the fingers of the rain,
To drink into my eyes the shine
Of every slanting silver line,
To catch the freshened, fragrant breeze
From drenched and dripping apple-trees.
For soon the shower will be done,
And then the broad face of the sun
Will laugh above the rain-soaked earth
Until the world with answering mirth
Shakes joyously, and each round drop
Rolls, twinkling, from its grass-blade top.
How can I bear it; buried here,
While overhead the sky grows clear
And blue again after the storm?
O, multi-colored, multiform,
Beloved beauty over me,
That I shall never, never see
Again!   Spring-silver, autumn-gold,
That I shall never more behold!

Sleeping your myriad magics through,
Close-sepulchred away from you!
O God, I cried, give me new birth,
And put me back upon the earth!
Upset each cloud's gigantic gourd
And let the heavy rain, down-poured
In one big torrent, set me free,
Washing my grave away from me!

I ceased; and through the breathless hush
That answered me, the far-off rush
Of herald wings came whispering
Like music down the vibrant string
Of my ascending prayer, and—crash!
Before the wild wind's whistling lash
The startled storm-clouds reared on high
And plunged in terror down the sky,
And the big rain in one black wave
Fell from the sky and struck my grave.
I know not how such things can be;
I only know there came to me
A fragrance such as never clings
To aught save happy living things;
A sound as of some joyous elf
Singing sweet songs to please himself,
And, through and over everything,
A sense of glad awakening.
The grass, a-tiptoe at my ear,
Whispering to me I could hear;
I felt the rain's cool finger-tips
Brushed tenderly across my lips,
Laid gently on my sealèd sight,
And all at once the heavy night

64

Fell from my eyes and I could see,—
A drenched and dripping apple-tree,
A last long line of silver rain,
A sky grown clear and blue again.
And as I looked a quickening gust
Of wind blew up to me and thrust
Into my face a miracle
Of orchard-breath, and with the smell,—
I know not how such things can be!—
I breathed my soul back into me.
Ah! Up then from the ground sprang I
And hailed the earth with such a cry
As is not heard save from a man
Who has been dead, and lives again.
About the trees my arms I wound;
Like one gone mad I hugged the ground;
I raised my quivering arms on high;
I laughed and laughed into the sky,
Till at my throat a strangling sob
Caught fiercely, and a great heart-throb
Sent instant tears into my eyes;
O God, I cried, no dark disguise
Can e'er hereafter hide from me
Thy radiant identity!
Thou canst not move across the grass
But my quick eyes will see Thee pass,
Nor speak, however silently,
But my hushed voice will answer Thee.
I know the path that tells Thy way
Through the cool eve of every day;

God, I can push the grass apart
And lay my finger on Thy heart!

The world stands out on either side
No wider than the heart is wide;
Above the world is stretched the sky,—
No higher than the soul is high.
The heart can push the sea and land
Farther away on either hand;
The soul can split the sky in two,
And let the face of God shine through.
But East and West will pinch the heart
That can not keep them pushed apart;
And he whose soul is flat—the sky
Will cave in on him by and by.

44

PART FOUR

Portrait by a Neighbor

Before she has her floor swept
  Or her dishes done,
Any day you'll find her
  A-sunning in the sun!

It's long after midnight
  Her key's in the lock,
And you never see her chimney smoke
  Till past ten o'clock!

She digs in her garden
  With a shovel and a spoon,
She weeds her lazy lettuce
  By the light of the moon.

She walks up the walk
  Like a woman in a dream,
She forgets she borrowed butter
  And pays you back cream!

Her lawn looks like a meadow,
  And if she mows the place
She leaves the clover standing
  And the Queen Anne's lace!

The Bean-Stalk

Ho, Giant! This is I!
I have built me a bean-stalk into your sky!
La,—but it's lovely, up so high!

This is how I came,—I put
Here my knee, there my foot,
Up and up, from shoot to shoot—
And the blessèd bean-stalk thinning
Like the mischief all the time,
Till it took me rocking, spinning,
In a dizzy, sunny circle,
Making angles with the root,
Far and out above the cackle
Of the city I was born in,
Till the little dirty city
In the light so sheer and sunny
Shone as dazzling bright and pretty
As the money that you find
In a dream of finding money—
What a wind! What a morning!—

Till the tiny, shiny city,
When I shot a glance below,
Shaken with a giddy laughter,
Sick and blissfully afraid,
Was a dew-drop on a blade,
And a pair of moments after
Was the whirling guess I made,—

And the wind was like a whip
Cracking past my icy ears,
And my hair stood out behind,
And my eyes were full of tears,
Wide-open and cold,
More tears than they could hold,
The wind was blowing so,
And my teeth were in a row,
Dry and grinning,
And I felt my foot slip,
And I scratched the wind and whined,
And I clutched the stalk and jabbered,
With my eyes shut blind,—
What a wind!   What a wind!

Your broad sky, Giant,
Is the shelf of a cupboard;
I make bean-stalks, I'm
A builder, like yourself,
But bean-stalks is my trade,
I couldn't make a shelf,
Don't know how they're made,
Now, a bean-stalk is more pliant—
La, what a climb!

Wraith

"Thin Rain, whom are you haunting,
   That you haunt my door?"
—Surely it is not I she's wanting;
   Some one living here before—
"Nobody's in the house but me:
You may come in if you like and see."

Thin as thread, with exquisite fingers,—
   Have you seen her, any of you?—
Grey shawl, and leaning on the wind,
   And the garden showing through?

Glimmering eyes,—and silent, mostly,
   Sort of a whisper, sort of a purr,
Asking something, asking it over,
   If you get a sound from her.—

Ever see her, any of you?—
   Strangest thing I've ever known,—
Every night since I moved in,
   And I came to be alone.

"Thin Rain, hush with your knocking!
   You may not come in!
This is I that you hear rocking;
   Nobody's with me, nor has been!"

Curious, how she tried the window,—
   Odd, the way she tries the door,—
Wonder just what sort of people
   Could have had this house before . . .

Lament

Listen, children:
Your father is dead.
From his old coats
I'll make you little jackets;
I'll make you little trousers
From his old pants.
There'll be in his pockets
Things he used to put there,
Keys and pennies
Covered with tobacco;
Dan shall have the pennies
To save in his bank;
Anne shall have the keys
To make a pretty noise with.
Life must go on,
And the dead be forgotten;
Life must go on,
Though good men die;
Anne, eat your breakfast;
Dan, take your medicine;
Life must go on;
I forget just why.

Tavern

I'll keep a little tavern
  Below the high hill's crest,
Wherein all grey-eyed people
  May set them down and rest.

There shall be plates a-plenty,
  And mugs to melt the chill
Of all the grey-eyed people
  Who happen up the hill.

There sound will sleep the traveller,
  And dream his journey's end,
But I will rouse at midnight
  The falling fire to tend.

Aye, 'tis a curious fancy—
  But all the good I know
Was taught me out of two grey eyes
  A long time ago.

When the Year Grows Old

I cannot but remember
  When the year grows old—
October—November—
  How she disliked the cold!

She used to watch the swallows
  Go down across the sky,
And turn from the window
  With a little sharp sigh.

And often when the brown leaves
  Were brittle on the ground,
And the wind in the chimney
  Made a melancholy sound,

She had a look about her
  That I wish I could forget—
The look of a scared thing
  Sitting in a net!

Oh, beautiful at nightfall
  The soft spitting snow!
And beautiful the bare boughs
  Rubbing to and fro!

But the roaring of the fire,
  And the warmth of fur,
And the boiling of the kettle
  Were beautiful to her!

I cannot but remember
    When the year grows old—
October—November—
    How she disliked the cold!

The Return from Town

As I sat down by Saddle Stream
  To bathe my dusty feet there
A boy was standing on the bridge
  Any girl would meet there.

As I went over Woody Knob
  And dipped into the hollow,
A youth was coming up the hill
  Any maid would follow.

Then in I turned at my own gate,—
  And nothing to be sad for—
To such a man as any wife
  Would pass a pretty lad for.

The Ballad of the Harp-Weaver

"Son," said my mother,
  When I was knee-high,
"You've need of clothes to cover you,
  And not a rag have I.

"There's nothing in the house
  To make a boy breeches,
Nor shears to cut a cloth with
  Nor thread to take stitches.

"There's nothing in the house
  But a loaf-end of rye,
And a harp with a woman's head
  Nobody will buy,"
  And she began to cry.

That was in the early fall.
  When came the late fall,
"Son," she said, "the sight of you
  Makes your mother's blood crawl,—

"Little skinny shoulder-blades
  Sticking through your clothes!
And where you'll get a jacket from
  God above knows.

"It's lucky for me, lad,
  Your daddy's in the ground,
And can't see the way I let
  His son go around!"
  And she made a queer sound.

That was in the late fall.
  When the winter came,
I'd not a pair of breeches
  Nor a shirt to my name.

I couldn't go to school,
  Or out of doors to play.
And all the other little boys
  Passed our way.

"Son," said my mother,
  "Come, climb into my lap,
And I'll chafe your little bones
  While you take a nap."

And, oh, but we were silly
  For half an hour or more,
Me with my long legs
  Dragging on the floor,

A-rock-rock-rocking
  To a mother-goose rhyme!
Oh, but we were happy
  For half an hour's time!

But there was I, a great boy,
  And what would folks say
To hear my mother singing me
  To sleep all day,
    In such a daft way?

Men say the winter
  Was bad that year;
Fuel was scarce,
  And food was dear.

A wind with a wolf's head
  Howled about our door,
And we burned up the chairs
  And sat upon the floor.

All that was left us
  Was a chair we couldn't break,
And the harp with a woman's head
  Nobody would take,
    For song or pity's sake.

The night before Christmas
  I cried with the cold,
I cried myself to sleep
  Like a two-year-old.

And in the deep night
  I felt my mother rise,
And stare down upon me
  With love in her eyes.

I saw my mother sitting
  On the one good chair,
A light falling on her
  From I couldn't tell where,

Looking nineteen,
    And not a day older,
And the harp with a woman's head
    Leaned against her shoulder.

Her thin fingers, moving
    In the thin, tall strings,
Were weav-weav-weaving
    Wonderful things.

Many bright threads,
    From where I couldn't see,
Were running through the harp-strings
    Rapidly,

And gold threads whistling
    Through my mother's hand.
I saw the web grow,
    And the pattern expand.

She wove a child's jacket,
    And when it was done
She laid it on the floor
    And wove another one.

She wove a red cloak
    So regal to see,
"She's made it for a king's son,"
    I said, "and not for me."
    But I knew it was for me.

She wove a pair of breeches
  Quicker than that!
She wove a pair of boots
  And a little cocked hat.

She wove a pair of mittens,
  She wove a little blouse,
She wove all night
  In the still, cold house.

She sang as she worked,
  And the harp-strings spoke;
Her voice never faltered,
  And the thread never broke.
  And when I awoke,—

There sat my mother
  With the harp against her shoulder,
Looking nineteen
  And not a day older,

A smile about her lips,
  And a light about her head,
And her hands in the harp-strings
  Frozen dead.

And piled up beside her
  And toppling to the skies,
Were the clothes of a king's son,
  Just my size.

PART FIVE

Memorial to D. C.

(VASSAR COLLEGE, *1918*)

Oh, loveliest throat of all sweet throats,
  Where now no more the music is,
With hands that wrote you little notes
  I write you little elegies!

Epitaph

Heap not on this mound
    Roses that she loved so well;
Why bewilder her with roses,
    That she cannot see or smell?
She is happy where she lies
With the dust upon her eyes.

Prayer to Persephone

Be to her, Persephone,
All the things I might not be;
Take her head upon your knee.
She that was so proud and wild,
Flippant, arrogant and free,
She that had no need of me,
Is a little lonely child
Lost in Hell,—Persephone,
Take her head upon your knee;
Say to her, "My dear, my dear,
It is not so dreadful here."

Chorus

Give away her gowns,
Give away her shoes;
She has no more use
For her fragrant gowns;
Take them all down,
Blue, green, blue,
Lilac, pink, blue,
From their padded hangers;
She will dance no more
In her narrow shoes;
Sweep her narrow shoes
From the closet floor.

Elegy

Let them bury your big eyes
In the secret earth securely,
Your thin fingers, and your fair,
Soft, indefinite-colored hair,—
All of these in some way, surely,
From the secret earth shall rise;
Not for these I sit and stare,
Broken and bereft completely;
Your young flesh that sat so neatly
On your little bones will sweetly
Blossom in the air.

But your voice,—never the rushing
Of a river underground,
Not the rising of the wind
In the trees before the rain,
Not the woodcock's watery call,
Not the note the white-throat utters,
Not the feet of children pushing
Yellow leaves along the gutters
In the blue and bitter fall,
Shall content my musing mind
For the beauty of that sound
That in no new way at all
Ever will be heard again.

Sweetly through the sappy stalk
Of the vigorous weed,
Holding all it held before,
Cherished by the faithful sun,
On and on eternally
Shall your altered fluid run,
Bud and bloom and go to seed;
But your singing days are done;
But the music of your talk
Never shall the chemistry
Of the secret earth restore.
All your lovely words are spoken.
Once the ivory box is broken,
Beats the golden bird no more.

Dirge

Boys and girls that held her dear,
 Do your weeping now;
All you loved of her lies here.

Brought to earth the arrogant brow,
 And the withering tongue
Chastened; do your weeping now.

Sing whatever songs are sung,
 Wind whatever wreath,
For a playmate perished young,

For a spirit spent in death.
Boys and girls that held her dear,
All you loved of her lies here.

PART SIX

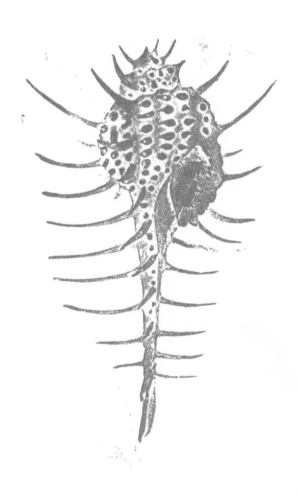

Sonnets

I

Mindful of you the sodden earth in spring,
And all the flowers that in the springtime grow,
And dusty roads, and thistles, and the slow
Rising of the round moon, all throats that sing
The summer through, and each departing wing,
And all the nests that the bared branches show,
And all winds that in any weather blow,
And all the storms that the four seasons bring.

You go no more on your exultant feet
Up paths that only mist and morning knew,
Or watch the wind, or listen to the beat
Of a bird's wings too high in air to view,—
But you were something more than young and sweet
And fair,—and the long year remembers you.

Oh, think not I am faithful to a vow!
Faithless am I save to love's self alone.
Were you not lovely I would leave you now:
After the feet of beauty fly my own.
Were you not still my hunger's rarest food,
And water ever to my wildest thirst,
I would desert you—think not but I would!—
And seek another as I sought you first.

But you are mobile as the veering air,
And all your charms more changeful than the tide,
Wherefore to be inconstant is no care:
I have but to continue at your side.
So wanton, light and false, my love, are you,
I am most faithless when I most am true.

III

And you as well must die, belovèd dust,
And all your beauty stand you in no stead;
This flawless, vital hand, this perfect head,
This body of flame and steel, before the gust
Of Death, or under his autumnal frost,
Shall be as any leaf, be no less dead
Than the first leaf that fell,—this wonder fled.
Altered, estranged, disintegrated, lost.

Nor shall my love avail you in your hour.
In spite of all my love, you will arise
Upon that day and wander down the air
Obscurely as the unattended flower,
It mattering not how beautiful you were,
Or how belovèd above all else that dies.

IV

Time does not bring relief; you all have lied
Who told me time would ease me of my pain!
I miss him in the weeping of the rain;
I want him at the shrinking of the tide;
The old snows melt from every mountain-side,
And last year's leaves are smoke in every lane;
But last year's bitter loving must remain
Heaped on my heart, and my old thoughts abide!

There are a hundred places where I fear
To go,—so with his memory they brim!
And entering with relief some quiet place
Where never fell his foot or shone his face
I say, "There is no memory of him here!"
And so stand stricken, so remembering him!

V

This door you might not open, and you did;
So enter now, and see for what slight thing
You are betrayed. . . . Here is no treasure hid,
No cauldron, no clear crystal mirroring
The sought-for truth, no heads of women slain
For greed like yours, no writhings of distress,
But only what you see. . . . Look yet again—
An empty room, cobwebbed and comfortless.

Yet this alone out of my life I kept
Unto myself, lest any know me quite;
And you did so profane me when you crept
Unto the threshold of this room to-night
That I must never more behold your face.
This now is yours.   I seek another place.

VI

Pity me not because the light of day
At close of day no longer walks the sky;
Pity me not for beauties passed away
From field and thicket as the year goes by;
Pity me not the waning of the moon,
Nor that the ebbing tide goes out to sea,
Nor that a man's desire is hushed so soon,
And you no longer look with love on me.

This have I known always: Love is no more
Than the wide blossom which the wind assails,
Than the great tide that treads the shifting shore,
Strewing fresh wreckage gathered in the gales;
Pity me that the heart is slow to learn
What the swift mind beholds at every turn.

Oh, oh, you will be sorry for that word!
Give back my book and take my kiss instead.
Was it my enemy or my friend I heard,
"What a big book for such a little head!"
Come, I will show you now my newest hat,
And you may watch me purse my mouth and prink!
Oh, I shall love you still, and all of that.
I never again shall tell you what I think.

I shall be sweet and crafty, soft and sly;
You will not catch me reading any more:
I shall be called a wife to pattern by;
And some day when you knock and push the door,
Some sane day, not too bright and not too stormy,
I shall be gone, and you may whistle for me.

VIII

I know I am but summer to your heart,
And not the full four seasons of the year;
And you must welcome from another part
Such noble moods as are not mine, my dear,
No gracious weight of golden fruits to sell
Have I, not any wise and wintry thing;
And I have loved you all too long and well
To carry still the high sweet breast of Spring.
Wherefore I say: O love, as summer goes,
I must be gone, steal forth with silent drums,
That you may hail anew the bird and rose
When I come back to you, as summer comes.
Else will you seek, at some not distant time,
Even your summer in another clime.

IX

I shall go back again to the bleak shore
And build a little shanty on the sand,
In such a way that the extremest band
Of brittle seaweed will escape my door
But by a yard or two; and nevermore
Shall I return to take you by the hand;
I shall be gone to what I understand,
And happier than I ever was before.

The love that stood a moment in your eyes,
The words that lay a moment on your tongue,
Are one with all that in a moment dies,
A little under-said and over-sung.
But I shall find the sullen rocks and skies
Unchanged from what they were when I was young.

X

Say what you will, and scratch my heart to find
The roots of last year's roses in my breast;
I am as surely riper in my mind
As if the fruit stood in the stalls confessed.
Laugh at the unshed leaf, say what you will,
Call me in all things what I was before,
A flutterer in the wind, a woman still;
I tell you I am what I was and more.

My branches weigh me down, frost cleans the air,
My sky is black with small birds bearing south;
Say what you will, confuse me with fine care,
Put by my word as but an April truth—
Autumn is no less on me than a rose
Hugs the brown bough and sighs before it goes.

Your face is like a chamber where a king
Dies of his wounds, untended and alone,
Stifling with courteous gesture the crude moan
That speaks too loud of mortal perishing,
Rising on elbow in the dark to sing
Some rhyme now out of season but well known
In days when banners in his face were blown
And every woman had a rose to fling.

I know that through your eyes which look on me
Who stand regarding you with pitiful breath,
You see beyond the moment's pause, you see
The sunny sky, the skimming bird beneath,
And, fronting on your windows hopelessly,
Black in the noon, the broad estates of Death.

XII

Here is a wound that never will heal, I know,
Being wrought not of a dearness and a death,
But of a love turned ashes and the breath
Gone out of beauty; never again will grow
The grass on that scarred acre, though I sow
Young seed there yearly and the sky bequeath
Its friendly weathers down, far underneath
Shall be such bitterness of an old woe.

That April should be shattered by a gust,
That August should be levelled by a rain,
I can endure, and that the lifted dust
Of man should settle to the earth again;
But that a dream can die, will be a thrust
Between my ribs forever of hot pain.

XIII

Euclid alone has looked on Beauty bare.
Let all who prate of Beauty hold their peace,
And lay them prone upon the earth and cease
To ponder on themselves, the while they stare
At nothing, intricately drawn nowhere
In shapes of shifting lineage; let geese
Gabble and hiss, but heroes seek release
From dusty bondage into luminous air.

O blinding hour, O holy, terrible day,
When first the shaft into his vision shone
Of light anatomized!   Euclid alone
Has looked on Beauty bare.   Fortunate they
Who, though once only and then but far away,
Have heard her massive sandal set on stone.